Basic
WOODWORKING

All the Skills and Tools You Need to Get Started

Cheryl Sobun, editor

Jim Bowman,
woodworker and consultant

Photographs by
Alan Wycheck

STACKPOLE
BOOKS

0 11557 03113 3

Copyright © 2004 by Stackpole Books

Published by
STACKPOLE BOOKS
5067 Ritter Road
Mechanicsburg, PA 17055
www.stackpolebooks.com

Printed in China

10 9 8 7 6 5 4 3 2 1

First edition

Cover design by Tracy Patterson

Library of Congress Cataloging-in-Publication Data

Basic woodworking : all the skills and tools you need to get started / Cheryl Sobun, editor ; Jim Bowman, woodworker and consultant ; photographs by Alan Wycheck.— 1st ed.
       p. cm.
  ISBN 0-8117-3113-8
  1. Woodwork. 2. Woodworking tools. I. Sobun, Cheryl.
TT180.B235 2004
684'.08—dc22

                                        2004014333

Contents

Acknowledgments

I would like to thank everyone who has helped make this book possible: Karlton Smith, my fiancé, for his unfailing support; Jim Bowman of Bowman's Custom Woodworking in Annville, Pennsylvania, for his time and assistance; Alan Wycheck of Wycheck Photography in Harrisburg, Pennsylvania, for so thoroughly capturing the art of woodworking on film; George Geissler, for additional expert information; and Judith Schnell and Mark Allison of Stackpole Books, for allowing me to set this project in motion.

—Cheryl Sobun

Introduction

If you're reading this, you have either decided to try your hand at woodworking or are seriously entertaining the idea. Perhaps a lifelong love of beautiful wood and craftsmanship sparked your interest in woodworking, or perhaps it was exorbitant furniture prices. Whatever the reason, you are probably feeling a bit overwhelmed. There are as many woodworking books and pieces of equipment on the market as there are shelves in a hardware store. What does a person really need to begin? What types of projects should a beginner attempt?

This book is intended to be an introduction to woodworking's fundamental tools, equipment, and techniques, for the beginner who has little to no familiarity with the subject. It should not be treated as exhaustive or all-encompassing. Working with wood involves a number of often-difficult skills that take years to master, and even specific subjects such as routing or painting can hardly be summed up in a single volume. It's best to think of this book as your first step into a much larger world.

The activities in this book have been designed with a "learn as you go" approach—you'll be encountering the woodworker's basic tools and techniques at the same time that you're creating a series of increasingly complex projects. You may find that your finished projects are sometimes not quite as professional-looking as those pictured in the book—perhaps your sanding is uneven in spots, or one of your bench's legs is shorter than the other. In these cases, remember that woodworking skill needs time and practice to develop—the more experience you have with the tools, and the more you come to understand the unique qualities of different types of wood, the better your work will look.

Do keep in mind that woodworking provides plenty of opportunity to injure oneself. Exercise great care at all times when carrying out these projects, especially when power tools are involved. Read all instructions in this book carefully, and be sure to also read the manufacturer's supplied instructions for all equipment that you use, with an eye to any safety precautions. It's critical that you pay attention to what you're doing at all times when working with wood, and that you use common sense.

1

Equipment and Materials

On the following pages are pictures and descriptions of the woodworking tools and materials you'll learn how to use by completing the projects in this book, as well as a few other optional pieces that you might want to include in your collection. It's best to build your collection gradually, making purchases only as necessary. Otherwise, the costs can become overwhelming, and you'll wind up having fancy tools you don't need.

Basic Woodworking Tools

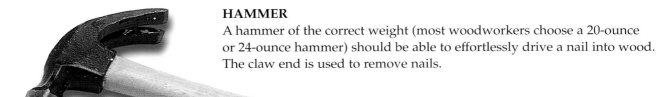

HAMMER
A hammer of the correct weight (most woodworkers choose a 20-ounce or 24-ounce hammer) should be able to effortlessly drive a nail into wood. The claw end is used to remove nails.

NAIL SET
Used to set the head of a finish nail below the surface of the wood.

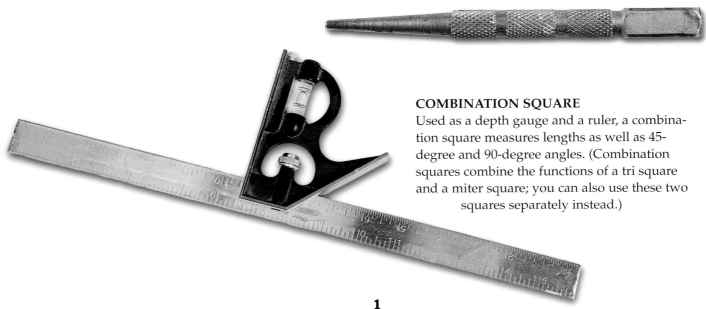

COMBINATION SQUARE
Used as a depth gauge and a ruler, a combination square measures lengths as well as 45-degree and 90-degree angles. (Combination squares combine the functions of a tri square and a miter square; you can also use these two squares separately instead.)

Using Power Tools Safely

Using power tools improperly can be extremely dangerous. It is important that you carefully read and understand the instructions that come with any power tool before you use it.

It is also important that you use eye protection—safety goggles or safety glasses made for shop use. You should always protect your eyes from the very real possibility of flying debris caused by the use of power tools.

Nearly everyone who works in a woodshop knows someone who was injured when a hand or finger came too close to a power tool, or vice versa. Good woodworkers are aware of where their hands are at all times. Fingers should always be kept at least 4 inches away from a blade or bit that has been turned on.

Hearing protection should always be used; even short exposure to the sound of loud power tools can cause hearing damage.

Cutting tools that are in good repair and used properly will always cut through wood quickly and easily. You should never have to force a blade through wood. If a blade is binding—being pinched by the wood—or a woodworking tool is not cutting easily, something is wrong. Turn the machine off and correct the problem by readjusting the wood or changing the blade.

SPEED SQUARE
A triangle-shaped square used to measure and check 90-degree and 45-degree angles.

POWER MITER SAW
A stationary electric saw used to cut wood, either straight on or at an angle. The wood is held at the bottom of the unit and the blade is brought down upon it.

TABLE SAW
A stationary electric saw that can cut wood straight on or at an angle. The wood is pushed along the surface toward the blade.

ASSORTED SAW BLADES

Various sizes and types of blades are available for use with the table and miter saws.

PUSH STICK

A safety tool used for pushing wood through a table saw, a push stick helps keep your hands away from the blade.

HAND-HELD JIGSAW AND BLADES

A jigsaw is excellent for making curved cuts, but it also makes straight and angled cuts. Note that while many woodworkers use the terms "jigsaw" and "saber saw" interchangeably, others differentiate the jigsaw as being the smaller of the two saws.

ROUTER

Routers have a bit sticking out of the bottom that is used to smooth, round, hollow out, or decorate wood. Standard (or "fixed") routers are best suited for work along the edges of a piece of wood. For work that is closer to the center of the wood, such as groove cutting, a plunge router is recommended instead.

ROUTER BITS
Attachments for the router are known as bits or cutters. Pictured here are just a few of the hundreds that can be used to put different edges or patterns, known as profiles, in wood. Many bits come equipped with guide bearings that help them to move smoothly over a surface. When changing a router bit, unplug the router, turn it upside down, and use a wrench to remove one bit and replace it with another.

PLUNGE ROUTER
Operates much the same as a regular router, but has a built-in base through which the bit can pass and "plunge" into the surface of the wood. Some combination routers are now available that feature a detachable base, allowing you to use the tool either as a fixed or plunge router.

BATTERY-POWERED DRILL
Quickly drills holes in wood, using a variety of bits and bit sizes. The battery-powered drill can also drive in screws and extract them. For the projects in this book, it's important to keep the drill perfectly perpendicular to the surface of the wood.

TAPERED BIT WITH COUNTERSINK
Used to drill holes for flathead wood screws. The bit is tapered to match the shape of a wood screw, while the countersink—the thick segment above the bit—cuts out a larger section for the head of the screw.

4

FORSTNER BIT

The forstner bit is also useful for flat-bottomed holes, as well as angled and overlapping cuts and holes that go all the way through the wood.

SCREWDRIVER

Puts screws into place and removes them. A set of individual screwdrivers works fine, of course, but a battery-powered one (shown here) and a set of bits make things much easier for not a lot of extra money.

HANDHELD PLANE

A handheld tool used to smooth and straighten the surface of a piece of wood, it can also round corners. The plane's blade must be razor-sharp and should cut *with* the direction of the wood grain, not against it.

TAPE MEASURE

A 12-foot or 15-foot tape will do for smaller projects. Use a longer one for larger wood projects.

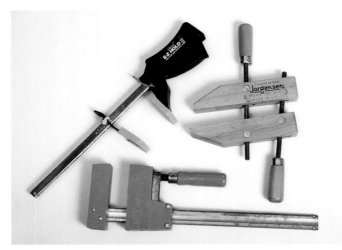

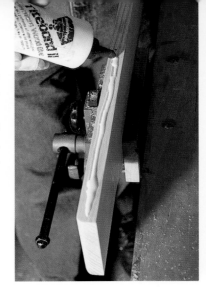

VISE
A vise is a fixture that is installed into your work surface. Like a clamp, it secures wood. A common style is shown in use here.

WOOD CLAMPS
Used to temporarily secure wood or hold it down on a table perfectly still while sawing, drilling, or sanding.

STRAIGHT-EDGE CLAMP
Clamps on to wood and creates a straight edge along which a router can move.

SANDPAPER
Used to smooth the surface of wood. Sandpaper comes in many grit sizes. Smaller sizes such as 50 or 60 are more abrasive. Higher sizes such as 220, 320, or 400, are much finer. Sanding jobs usually start with a more abrasive grade and end with a finer grade. For many woodworking projects you can use a 120-grit sandpaper, a medium grade, to start and a 220-grit sandpaper, a fine grade, to finish.

SANDPAPER BLOCK
Wrapping sandpaper around a small piece of wood makes hand sanding easier. You can also purchase sandpaper blocks made of cork, hard foam, or other materials, some of which can bend around curved areas.

WOODEN PLUGS
Used to plug screw holes, wooden plugs can be sanded, finished, and painted.

FINISH NAILS
Finish nails have much smaller heads than standard nails. They're good for concealing in wood because they can be driven below the wood's surface with a nail set.

WOOD SCREWS
Used to hold wood together. Screws vary in type, gauge, length, and shank thickness. *Type* refers to the kind of head: flatheads do not stick above the surface at all, oval heads protrude slightly, and round heads extend even further. *Gauges* are based on the diameter of the screw head. They range from 0 to 20, with 20 being the thickest; the most common are 6, 8, and 10. The thicker the gauge and the longer the screw, the stronger the hold. *Shank thickness* refers to the thickness of the screw between the head and the thread, which will determine the size of the drill bit you will need to create a hole for the screw.

UTILITY KNIFE
Keep a utility knife on hand for assorted cutting.

PUTTY KNIFE
Used to get glue or old paint off of wood, a putty knife is also good for forcing wood filler into holes and cracks.

HAND SCRAPER
If you're unable to remove all of the glue from a piece of wood, use a hand scraper to take off the remnants.

WOODWORKING GLUE
Used to hold pieces of wood together, woodworking glue can be used alone or with nails or screws. A glue that is 100 percent waterproof is required for some woodworking projects, such as the cutting board in Chapter 2.

GLUE BRUSH
Used for applying glue to wood.

PENCIL
Used to mark out lines and measurements.

GLOVES
Gloves should be worn when handling varnishes, stains, some types of glue, and other substances.

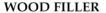

WOOD FILLER
Used to fill in and smooth over a hole after finish nails are pounded in, or to fill cracks and holes in the wood. Wood filler is available in a variety of shades. Try to find as close a color match as possible to the wood you're working with.

FLAT STICK
Keep one on hand for spreading glue, wood filler, and other substances.

TACK CLOTHS AND LINT-FREE CLOTHS
Tack cloths remove dust from wood after sanding. Lint-free cloths are used to apply varnishes and stains.

PAINT BRUSHES

Used to apply varnishes, primers, and paint to wood. Use larger brushes for larger surface areas and smaller brushes for smaller or hard-to-reach areas.

FINISH

Protects wood and enhances its appearance. A finish is applied after a wood project is completed. There are many different types of finishes available, including oils, varnishes, shellacs, and lacquers. Finishes generally come in either clear or tinted varieties. A clear finish is used if you want to preserve the natural wood color, while a tinted finish colors the wood.

FRENCH CURVE

A design tool used to help draw curves.

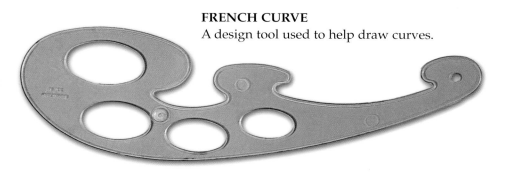

QUARTER-INCH PLYWOOD

You'll need to have some spare plywood on hand to create the template used for the shelf in Chapter 4.

WOODEN PEGS

Pegs can be found in a variety of styles and sizes. The Shaker-style pegs pictured here are $3\frac{1}{2}$ inches long with a $\frac{7}{8}$-inch head; they are used for the peg shelf project in Chapter 4.

Some Woodworking Extras

ORBITAL SANDER

A handheld random-orbit electric sander works with all grades of sandpaper and makes smoothing large projects much easier. Either orbital or hand sanding will work for the projects in this book.

HAND SAW

A traditional hand saw may be used instead of a miter saw for straight or angled cuts. Hand saws are sometimes more convenient for smaller jobs, but they are less precise and give a rougher cut than a miter saw.

PLUG CUTTERS

Can be used to cut your own wooden plugs if you'd rather make them instead of buying them.

A Safe Workspace

A corner of a basement, shed, or garage makes an ideal place to do woodworking—a garage especially because it's easy to ventilate. You might even find it practical to set up a work table outside, as long as there's no rain in the forecast and you have an electrical outlet nearby. Make certain all outlets in your workspace are properly grounded and can handle the load of the tools.

No matter where you choose to work, you'll need to have access to a sturdy work surface, around 3 feet by 6 feet and a couple of inches thick, upon which you can hammer and saw wood and to which you can attach clamps and a vise.

Many pieces of electrical woodworking equipment, such as routers and orbital sanders, will have a built-in dust extraction system or the ability to connect to one. For the beginner, these built-in dust extraction systems—coupled with proper ventilation and, ideally, a dust mask—will suffice. As you become more serious about woodworking, you might want to consider investing in a stand-up vacuum system, for example, which will more thoroughly collect sawdust and chips. An industrial vacuum cleaner is another option that works wonderfully for general workshop cleaning. You will need to make sure your workshop is as clean and free from sawdust and wood chips as possible, not only for your health, but because the material can be a fire hazard. Be sure to equip your workshop with a smoke alarm and fire extinguisher.

TWIST DRILL BIT
The most common type of bit, twist drill bits can be used for both wood and metal.

BRAD POINT BIT
The brad point bit resembles the twist bit—the familiar, twisting bit most often associated with the drill—but creates flat-bottomed holes and has a point on the end for more accurate drilling.

DRILL PRESS
A stationary tool used to drill holes in wood, this can be used instead of a handheld drill. Drilling tends to be more accurate with a drill press.

11

Common Types of Wood

There are hundreds of different types of wood available for use in woodworking projects. They vary widely in their hardness, durability, texture, color, appearance, grain pattern, cost, and availability. Experienced woodworkers regularly use a few common types that are relatively easy to work with, beautiful to look at, and readily available. Eight of these varieties are described here. The type of wood you choose depends on the demands of the project you're making and on your individual taste. Learning the characteristics of the most common types of wood will help you make the best choice.

Some common terms to know:

Grain refers to the size, shape, and alignment of fibers in a piece of wood.

Figure refers to the pattern on a wood surface, which is determined by both natural growth patterns and the method by which the wood was cut.

Fiddleback is a wavy grain pattern.

Crotch refers to dramatic grain swirls in the wood.

Bird's-eye is a figure composed of small, rounded areas caused by indentations in some of the wood layers. These are not the same as *knots* in the wood, which occur where a tree branch once intersected the wood.

A *burl* is a wart-like growth that creates an unusual grain pattern. Burls often occur near or contain a knot or crotch.

Interlocked refers to grain that gradually reverses direction several times as a tree adds its annual growth rings.

The easiest way to get wood for the projects in this book is to buy a finished piece cut to order at a lumberyard or home improvement retailer. This way your wood will start out smooth, flat, and ready to use. Rough wood is coarse and uneven and might be bowed. If you have the right tools, you can flatten and smooth rough wood for your projects. For beginners, however, it's best to start with finished wood.

CHERRY

Grows mainly in southeastern Canada and throughout the eastern half of the United States. Cherry heartwood, the mature wood that forms the spine of the tree, is a medium red-brown with its own characteristic luster. The grain is straight and finely textured, usually with a gently waving figure. Cherry has a natural tendency to darken over time to a beautiful, rich red. It is generally used for making fine furniture, cabinets, musical instruments, interiors, and cabinetwork.

RED OAK

Generally grows in the southern mountain regions, the Atlantic coastal plains, the central states, and southeastern Canada. The heartwood is reddish brown and coarse-grained. Red oak is generally used for flooring, furniture, cabinetry, and millwork.

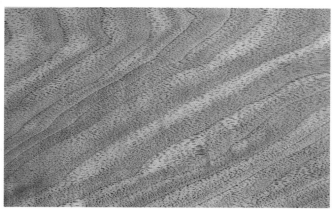

WALNUT

Grows from southern Canada down into Texas and Louisiana, across the coastal Carolinas, and along the coast to southern New York. This is America's premium furniture wood. The heartwood varies from purplish brown with darker veins to a grayish brown. The grain tends to be widely spaced and straight, but some highly figured walnut features fiddleback, burls, and crotch, with coarse-textured grain. Walnut is a favorite for furniture, bowls, paneling, musical instruments, veneer, and firearm stocks and grips.

YELLOW POPLAR

Grows from Connecticut to Florida and west to the Mississippi River. The greatest production is in the South and Southwest. The heartwood is a yellowish brown and is usually streaked with green, purple, black, blue, or red. It has a very straight grain and is uniform in texture. It is easy to work with, is inexpensive, paints well, and can be stained to resemble walnut or cherry. This lumber is used primarily for furniture, boxes, pallets, musical instruments, and interior finish trim and moldings.

HARD MAPLE

Grows in the eastern half of Canada, the northeastern United States, Appalachia, and parts of the Midwest. The texture is fine and very uniform. The grain is usually straight with little figure but can exhibit different patterns such as fiddleback and bird's-eye. This wood is generally used for lumber and veneer, with much going into flooring and furniture.

MAHOGANY

Grows in West, Central, and East Africa. The heartwood ranges from light to deep reddish brown and has excellent workability. The wood has moderately coarse texture and is straight-grained or interlocked. It is generally used for fine furniture and cabinetwork.

WHITE PINE
Grows mainly in Idaho but also in Montana, Oregon, and Washington. The heartwood varies from a cream color to light red-brown that darkens with exposure to light and air. The wood is generally straight-grained and easy to work with. It is used for building construction, siding, and interior and exterior trim.

BASSWOOD
Grows in the mid-Atlantic and central states. The heartwood is generally pale yellow-brown with some darker streaks. It is a soft wood, light in weight, and has a fine, even texture. It is straight-grained and very easy to work with. This wood is the premier choice of most woodcarvers because it holds details very well. It is often used to make Christmas tree ornaments, utensils, food containers, and Venetian blinds.

2

Making a Cutting Board

- **Measuring and marking**
- **Using a power miter saw**
- **Using a table saw**
- **Gluing and clamping**
- **Using a jigsaw**
- **Using a router**
- **Sanding and finishing**

The instructions for making this cutting board are designed to familiarize you with a number of fundamental tools and skills. When you're done, you'll have seen your first woodworking project through from start to finish, and you'll also have a practical piece you can use at home.

Because you'll be slicing food on the cutting board, it will need to be able to withstand numerous washings in soap and water. It's best to use a wood that is fairly nonporous—one with a tight grain. Hard maple, used here, is an excellent choice that has naturally contrasting colors in the grain, making for an attractive finished piece. Other good alternatives are oak and walnut.

The cutting board will be made up of ten blocks of wood that are 13 inches by 1 inch by 1 inch. After the blocks are assembled, the length of the board will be trimmed down to 12 inches. The finished cutting board will be 12 inches long, 10 inches wide, and 1 inch thick. This means you must start with a piece of maple that's at least 40 inches long and 5 inches wide and exactly 1 inch thick.

15

1. Use the tape measure to measure 13 inches from one end of the board and make a mark, then measure another 13 inches from that mark and make another mark. Another 13 inches and a third mark will give you three 13-inch segments.

2. Line up the edge of the combination square (or tri square) with the first mark, holding the handle of the square firmly against the side of the board.

3. Draw a line along the square. Repeat at the two other marks.

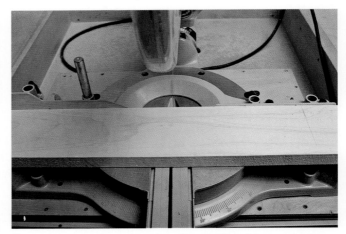

4. The marked-up wood will look like this, ready for sawing. If you wish, you can use a jigsaw, or even a hand saw, to cut these 13-inch lengths. (For this project, these first three cuts don't have to be exact, since you will be trimming off the excess with a miter saw later in the process.)

How to Use a Power Miter Saw

Before working with the miter saw, be sure to review the sidebar on page 2 for general guidelines on using power tools safely.

To use a power miter saw properly, first make certain that you're using a sharp blade and that the blade is tightly fastened. Use the proper blade—if, for example, you're cross-cutting wood (cutting across the grain) you should use what's known as a combination blade. When the blade is in place, the teeth at the bottom should be pointing toward the tool's backstop; this way the cutting action of the blade drives the wood downward instead of upward. Place the wood in the saw with the back edge resting firmly against the backstop and the bottom of the wood resting firmly on the base. Never cut twisted or rough wood with a miter saw—the two surfaces of the wood that are in contact with the machine need to be perfectly flat and finished so the wood can be held firmly in place as you cut. If you are cutting a long piece of wood—one that hangs well over the edges of the tool's base—make certain that the overhanging length is supported. It should not be left to dangle.

Once the wood is against the backstop bring the blade down—with the machine off—and adjust the wood until the side of the blade is just barely to the side of the pencil line, away from the section that you intend to cut from the main board. (This side of the board is referred to as the "waste" side, though it doesn't mean the remaining wood has to be discarded—it will be left over after you cut your section from the board. Whenever you use a saw, it's recommended that you cut just to the waste side of your pencil line, since the blade will end up removing a little bit of wood on either side of the saw.)

Push the blade up away from the wood, then turn the machine on. Make certain that the blade has reached full speed before it comes in contact with the wood. If you turn the machine on when the blade is touching the wood, the lumber might kick up into your face. Hold the wood in place with one hand, but keep both hands at least 4 inches away from the spinning blade at all times—remember that woodworkers should always be aware of where their hands are. With the other hand, bring the blade down and cut the wood completely, then turn the machine off. Never reach for the wood until the blade has stopped spinning.

5. Put on safety glasses—you should always wear safety glasses whenever you use woodworking machinery—and place the wood against the backstop of the power miter saw.

6. With the saw turned off, bring the blade down to the wood and adjust the wood so that the near side of the blade is lined up just to the waste side of the pencil line. (Note that the wood you cut off won't really be wasted; you will use it again. When you cut the additional pieces from it, just be certain that you always cut on the waste side.)

17

7. Push the blade back up, hold the wood firmly against the backstop, and turn the machine on. When the blade reaches full speed, bring it down on the wood and make your cut.

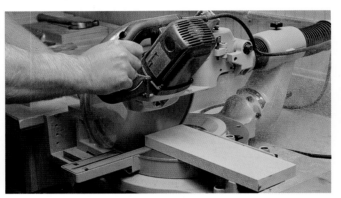

8. Cut through the entire piece of wood. Turn the machine off. Don't grab the wood until the blade has stopped spinning. Repeat this process at the other 13-inch marks.

9. The next step is to cut the wood into 1-inch strips using the table saw. You will need at least ten strips when you are finished. Since you have 5 inches to work with on each 13-inch section, you should have more than enough wood if you measure properly. Carefully measure out 1 inch between the blade and the table saw's fence—don't include the width of the blade in your measurement. Set the blade at 1 inch. A glue-line ripping blade (used here) makes a very smooth cut.

10. Hold the push stick against the wood using your right hand as shown; your left hand should keep the wood pressed firmly against the fence as the blade travels through the wood.

11. Turn the machine on and, using the push stick, push the wood toward the saw. Be careful to keep both hands well clear of the blade.

12. Push the wood completely past the blade, making certain the entire length has been cut. Turn the machine off.

How to Use a Table Saw

The table saw blade should be sharp and tightly fastened according to the tool's instructions, and the teeth should point in the same direction that the blade spins. The blade's height should be set so that the blade is sticking up no more than $1/4$ inch of above the wood. As shown in Step 10, it's a good idea to use a push stick when you're ripping (cutting with the grain) long pieces of wood on a table saw. If the piece you're cutting extends beyond the surface of the table saw, make certain that it is supported somehow; sawhorses or scrap furniture will work well. Whether or not you use a push stick, *never* put your hands closer to the blade than 4 inches when the machine is on. Most table saws come equipped with a blade guard that prevents the user from making contact with the blade (it's been removed in these photographs for the sake of clarity). Nonetheless, it's a good idea to follow these precautions even when a guard is in place.

Some experts recommend that if you are cutting a narrow strip of wood, the table saw should be set so that the width of the wood that will pass between the blade and the fence is greater than the width of the wood that will pass on the opposite side of the blade. Never run twisted, bowed, or rough wood through a table saw. Such wood can easily buck or kick back at you.

To use a table saw, set the wood in place before the block, keeping the edge pressed firmly against the fence. Don't let the blade touch the wood. Position yourself slightly to one side of the blade: you want to avoid being directly in line with it as you cut so that if the wood kicks back (or if any foreign matter in the wood is thrown out when it hits the blade) you are not directly in the line of fire. Turn the machine on, and when the blade is spinning at full speed, push the wood into it, keeping the edge of the wood pressed against the fence. When the wood is clear of the blade, turn off the machine. You should never pull the wood back through the machine, especially when it's turned on.

Table saws also feature a miter gauge—an adjustable backstop that allows you to cut wood at an angle. Although the projects in this book don't require the use of a miter gauge (and none is shown here) when you *do* cut wood with the assistance of a miter gauge, it is important that the wood maintains contact only with the gauge and the blade—it should never be in contact with the gauge, the blade, and the fence at the same time. If you cut when you have this three-point contact, there is a good chance the wood will kick back at you.

13. Move the big piece back to the front of the blade and repeat the process on the rest of the cut piece and the other two 13-inch segments. Never pull the wood back through the saw, especially if the machine is on.

14. You will now have ten or more wooden blocks that measure at least 13 inches by 1 inch by 1 inch. Note that some blocks will be longer than others, depending on how long the original board was.

15. Next, set up two wood clamps at about $11^{1}/_{2}$ inches apart.

You want the clamps open enough that all ten blocks can fit between them.

16. You should first do a dry run before gluing to make certain you have a smooth, flat, even fit. Set the pieces next to each other inside the clamp.

17. Very slight imperfections can be eliminated during sanding, but if one particular block is uneven or out of line, you should replace it with one of the leftover 13-inch pieces.

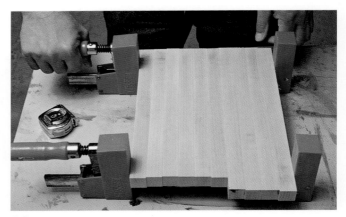

18. Tighten the clamps.

The wood should be firmly pressed together, but the clamps shouldn't be so tight that they cut into the wood.

19. Look at the surface of the board and run your fingers along it to make sure you have a smooth fit.

20. Loosen the clamps and remove the blocks.

21. Now it's time to glue the blocks together. For the particular glue used here—a powerful polyurethane called Gorilla Glue—the manufacturer suggests wetting lightly with water one of the two surfaces that are to be glued together. A spray bottle filled with tap water works well to spritz the wood. A number of wood glue brands require this step; be sure to check the label. No matter what brand you use to assemble the cutting board, make certain the glue is 100 percent waterproof.

22. Wipe each piece of wood you've spritzed to dry up excess moisture. The wood should be slightly damp, not dripping wet.

23. As this is an especially strong glue, you should put on a pair of gloves before using it. Apply the glue to the sides of the block opposite the sides that were spritzed. Don't put glue on the wetted sides, and don't glue any side that will be touching the clamps.

24. Spread the glue evenly, using a flat stick.

25. Place the wood blocks back into the clamp, pressing the damp sides against the glued sides.

26. Tighten the clamps.

27. The glue will ooze through the seams—this is to be expected. Let the cutting board dry for however long the glue manufacturer suggests, usually at least 24 hours.

22

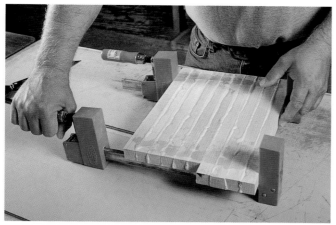

28. When the piece has had time to dry completely, unscrew the clamps . . .

. . . and remove the board.

29. The dried glue will look something like this.

30. Removing the excess glue is the next step, but before you do this, you need to create a sturdy brace against which you can set the board so it will not move while you work. If you don't have one in place, a brace can easily be made by screwing a straight piece of scrap lumber onto the work surface.

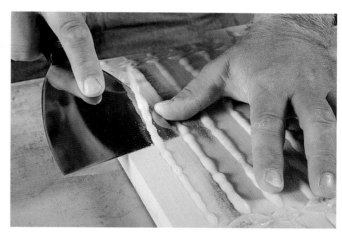

31. Place the board against the brace. With a putty knife, scrape off the excess glue, being careful not to gouge the wood with the edges of the blade.

The knife should be almost horizontal; don't hold it up vertically.

Push the knife away from you, toward the brace.

32. The putty knife will remove most of the glue, but you'll need to use a wood scraper to remove the last remnants. Use both hands to hold the two edges of the scraper and bow it in the center with your thumbs.

33. Hold the edge of the scraper against the wood and push the blade forward, away from you, toward the brace.

34. Keep the scraper bowed with your thumbs as you scrape. Scrape the entire front and back of the board (but not the edges) removing all traces of glue.

35. This is what the board will look like when you've finished scraping.

Tips on Sanding

For nearly every woodworking project you do, sanding will be required at some point. There are numerous types and grades of sandpaper available, but the following tips and techniques are for the most part universal:

- Always sand with the grain of the wood, not against it.
- It's best to have several grades of sandpaper on hand. Use at least two or three different grades for each project, moving from coarse to fine. For most of the projects in this book, a combination of 120 and 220 is recommended.
- Sandpaper wears down over time. When using a sanding block, rotate the paper over the block as it becomes dull, until the entire sheet is used up.
- Humidity reduces the effectiveness of sandpaper as well. Always store your paper in airtight containers when not in use.
- As your sandpaper becomes clogged with sawdust, clean it with a brush or vacuum.
- After sanding, always clear the project's surfaces with a tack cloth or damp sponge before finishing.
- When sanding hard-to-reach places, try using an emery board or wrapping sandpaper around a dowel.
- If you're using an orbital sander, don't press down on the tool. The sander's own weight will provide adequate pressure.

36. Now sand the entire board, front and back, smoothing the whole surface (once again, you can skip the edges). Start with 120-grade paper, followed by 220-grade paper. You can use a piece of sandpaper wrapped around a block . . .

. . . or an orbital sander.

37. The surface of the cutting board should now be smooth to the touch.

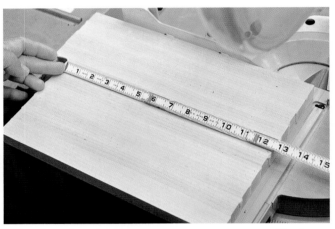

38. Next, keeping your tape measure perpendicular to one of the ends, measure and mark a 12-inch section between the two ends of the board (in those places where the board is 13 inches long, this will be approximately ¹/₂ inch from either side).

39. Using the square, draw lines at the marks at both ends of the board.

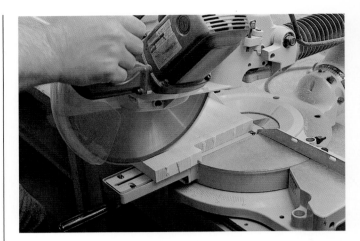

40. Use the power miter saw to cut off the excess length so your cutting board is exactly 12 inches long.

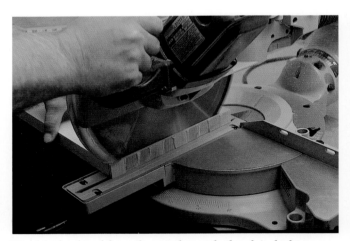

The blade should easily cut through the dried glue.

41. Next, you'll need to round off the corners of the board. With a quarter and a pencil, draw an arc on each of the corners.

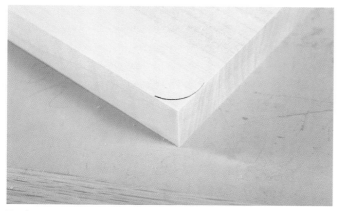

Each arc should be of the same length. You can determine this by measuring the distance from the corner of the board to the point where the arc intersects the side.

42. Use two bar clamps to secure the board to the work surface. These clamps are padded—if yours aren't, place a small piece of scrap wood between the clamps and the sanded board's surface to protect it. The board's surface should not be directly touching the clamps. Tighten the clamps so the wood will not move.

43. Using a jigsaw, cut along the pencil lines to round off all four corners. See the sidebar for detailed instructions on jigsaw use.

How to Use a Jigsaw

Two of the most common mistakes beginners make when using a handheld jigsaw are not supporting the wood properly and not leaving adequate clearance for the moving blade underneath the work surface. If you're cutting wood that's clamped to a work table, make sure the clamps are tight and that you're using enough of them to hold the wood as it's cut. A vise will work if you're just cutting the end off a piece of wood, but if you try to cut the part of the wood that's between the table and the vise, you will almost certainly bind—and possibly snap—the blade.

Make certain the jigsaw blade is sharp and fastened tightly in the machine. The teeth of the blade should point down toward the base of the saw. To cut, set the base of the saw (the tool should be off) on the wood and line up the inside edge of the blade with the "waste" side of the pencil line. Don't let the blade touch the wood until the machine is turned on. When it is, and the blade is moving at full speed, begin cutting. As you cut, make certain that the base of the saw always maintains full contact with the wood surface. Don't tip or tilt the saw.

If you're cutting a tight curve and the blade starts to bind, turn the machine off immediately. You're probably trying to cut too tight a radius with too large a blade; switch to a smaller one. Likewise, if the blade hits something on the underside of the wood, turn the saw off immediately and clear the obstacle.

When you're done with the cut, turn the machine off. Don't remove the blade from the wood until the blade is completely stopped. The wood could bounce if you do. Lay the handheld jigsaw on its side when it's not in use.

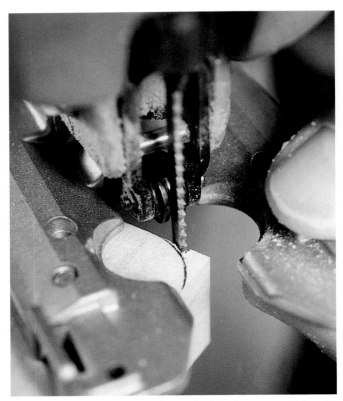

Be sure that the blade is aligned with the waste side of the pencil line.

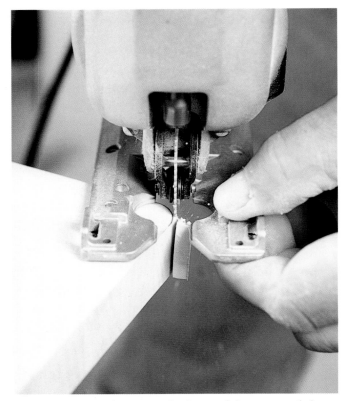

Maintain contact between the base of the saw and the wood surface at all times.

44. Remove the board from the clamps.

45. Sand the corners smooth. Hand sanding works best here—use 120-grade paper first, followed by 220-grade.

46. The next step is to round over all the edges of the board. You can use an electric router with a $^3/_8$-inch roundover bit (shown here) or a handheld planer to do this. Rounding over the edges with sandpaper is another option, but doing so takes a great deal of elbow grease and care to see that the edges remain even. Refer to the sidebar on page 29 for instructions on using a router.

47. Clamp the wood to the work surface again. Place the router on top of the wood.

48. Position the bit near the edge of the wood, keeping the router base flat on the wood surface. Don't let the bit touch the wood.

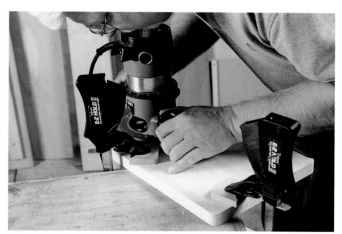

49. Turn the router on and move the bit into the wood.

How to Use a Router

To use a router properly, the wood you're routing must be held securely to the work surface and properly supported, and the base of the router must be supported by the wood. If you're routing the edge of a thin piece of wood that is smaller than the router's base, place a piece of scrap wood next to the good wood so that the entire base of the tool is supported. The router bit, or cutter, must be fastened tightly in the router and set to the proper depth.

If you're using a straight-edge clamp as a guide for the router (as you will for the projects in Chapters 3 and 4), you simply need to make certain that the clamp is set at the correct distance so that the router base will ride along the guide to cut at the right place. To cut, hold the router in place, with the bit not touching the wood. Turn the machine tool on, let the bit rotation reach full speed, and begin cutting. You should always move the router from left to right or counterclockwise as you cut, opposite the direction in which the bit is spinning. If you move it in the same direction in which the bit is spinning, the tool could skip.

As you cut, make certain the base of the router maintains full contact with the surface of the wood. Run the router along the guide, but don't press it too tightly—doing so could burn or dent the wood. When the cut is complete, turn the machine off, wait for the bit to stop, and pull the tool away from the wood.

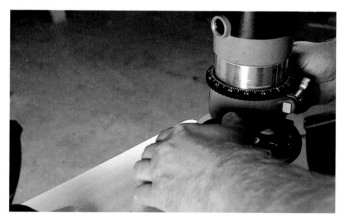

50. Move the router along the entire perimeter of the piece. The router bit's bearing will ride along the edge of the wood.

Don't press into the wood. Keep the router base flat against the wood surface as you move the tool.

It's important to keep the router moving while it is cutting. If you linger too long in one spot, you could burn the edge. Slight burns like this won't ruin your project because they can usually be sanded off, but deeper burns may be difficult or impossible to remove.

51. As an alternative to using a router, you can use a standard hand block plane. To start, set the blade at a shallow depth and try it out on a piece of scrap wood. Plane with or across the grain of the wood, not against it. If the plane gouges or sticks, too much blade may be sticking out of the bottom, or the blade may be too dull—it needs to be razor-sharp to work properly.

52. Carefully plane the board, with the bottom of the plane held at an angle to the edges. Don't let the plane wobble as it cuts, and remove only a little bit of wood at a time. You may find it helpful to clamp the board to your work surface.

53. When all the edges, front and back, have been rounded over, remove the board from the clamps and smooth all the rounded edges you've just made with sandpaper.

Use 120-grade paper first, then 220-grade.

You can either sand by hand or use an orbital sander. Slight burns left over from routing can usually be removed at this stage.

54. The last step in making the cutting board is to create a groove along one side. This groove will serve as a handle. Mark the board 1 inch in from the edge of one of the long sides of the board to indicate where the groove will go. Start the measurement at the vertical side of the wood, not at the end of the rounded edge.

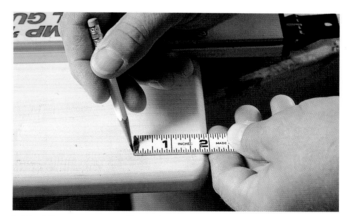

55. The groove will end 2 inches from each of the board's shorter sides. Make a 2-inch mark on each side, in line with the first mark you made. Again, measure from the side of the wood, not the rounded edge.

56. Using a combination square, measure 3½ inches in from the long side of the board that will receive the groove. Make a pencil mark.

57. Line up a straight-edge clamp at this mark and tighten it onto the wood.

58. With the straight-edge clamp in place, secure the board firmly to the work surface with wood clamps. Use scrap wood to protect the sanded surface of the board if necessary.

59. Attach a 1/2-inch radius bit to a plunge router and set the machine for a depth of 3/8 inch.

60. Place the base of the plunge router right up against the edge of the straight-edge clamp. The clamp will not move, allowing you to hold the router steady and move it along a straight line. Line up the bit so that its outside edge aligns with the 2-inch mark at one end of the board. Turn the router on, bring the bit down into the wood, and move the router steadily along the guide to the other 2-inch mark. Be sure not to press too hard against the guide or linger in one spot for very long. Stop as soon as you reach the mark and turn the machine off.

61. This is what the finished groove will look like.

62. Smooth the routed groove with 120-grade and 220-grade sandpaper, removing pencil marks and burn marks as necessary.

32

63. Using a tack cloth, wipe the board free of dust. Wipe both sides, all the edges, and the inside of the groove. Place a cloth between the board and the work surface to help keep the board from getting dusty or dinged during the finishing process.

64. You will complete the cutting board by applying two or three coats of a non-toxic finish, such as the Salad Bowl Finish by Mohawk used here.

65. Wipe the finish onto the board using a clean, lint-free cloth. It's best to wear gloves when applying any finish.

66. Make certain you cover the board's edges and the inside of the groove. Allow each coat of finish to dry thoroughly before applying the next coat. The label of the finish you use will specify drying time.

67. Thin strips of scrap wood will keep the freshly finished board up off the work surface so it can dry completely without sticking.

3

Making a Small Bench

- Creating and cutting a curve
- Cutting a dado
- Hammering and setting nails
- Using wood filler
- Priming and painting

This decorative piece is a more demanding project than the cutting board, as it entails joining pieces of wood at an angle to one another and making more complex cuts. You'll also become acquainted with some new tools and find new applications for those you've already used.

All the pieces needed for the bench can be cut from a single board that's 49 or more inches long, 7 1/2 inches wide, and 3/4 inch thick. White pine is used here—it's a good choice because it's lightweight, easy to cut, and holds paint very well.

35

1. To begin, measure in 14 inches from one of the short sides of the board and mark it with a pencil. Use the square to draw a line through the mark.

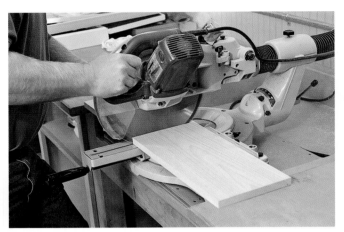

2. Put on your safety glasses. Place the wood on the miter saw with the long side pressed against the saw stop. Cut the board along the line you drew. The 14-inch-long piece will form the seat of the bench.

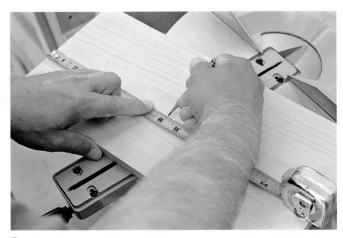

3. On the wood that is left, measure and mark 8 inches in from the short side, then measure and mark another 8-inch length from the first mark.

4. Draw straight lines through the two marks and cut the board with the miter saw along the two lines. These two 8-inch-long pieces will form the bench's legs. The remaining piece needs to be exactly 18 inches long; measure its length and cut off any excess with the miter saw. From this piece, measure and cut three pieces of wood that are each 1 1/2 inches wide and 18 inches long.

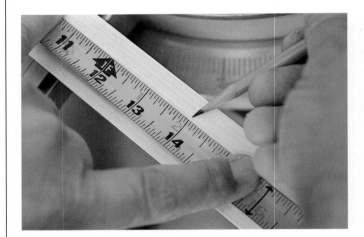

5. Measure, mark, and cut two of the 1 1/2-by-18-inch pieces down to 14 inches. These two pieces will form the sides of the bench. Set these two pieces and the third 18-inch-long piece aside.

6. On one of the 8-by-7½-inch pieces, use the combination square to make a mark 4½ inches in from the 7½-inch side. Then place the combination square against the 8-inch side and draw a short line along this mark in the middle of the board.

7. Measure in along the bottom of the piece and make marks 2 inches from both of the 8-inch sides.

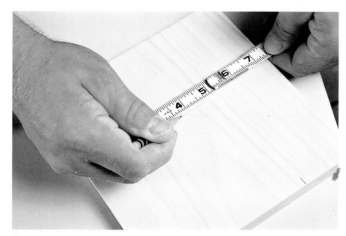

8. Next, measure along the line in the middle of the board to find a point 3¾ inches from the 8-inch side, and make a mark that bisects the line. This mark should be equidistant from both 8-inch sides.

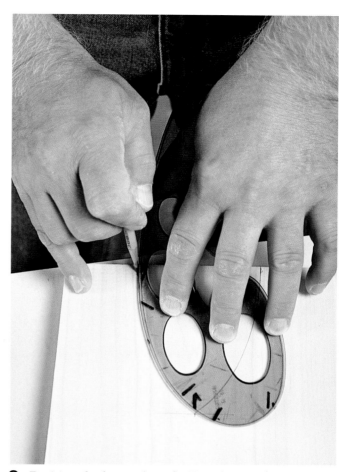

9. Position the long edge of a French curve on one of the 2-inch marks so that the curve crosses the center of the mark you made in Step 8. Trace along the edge of the curve to create one side of the arc. Turn the curve over and do the same to create the other side of the arc.

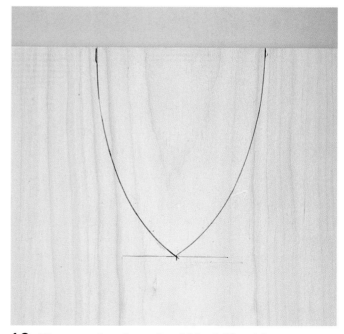

10. The completed arc should look like this.

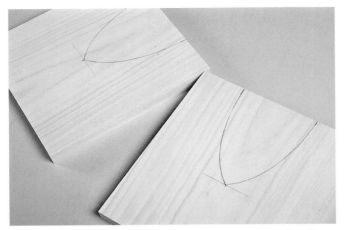

11. Measure, mark, and draw an arc on the other leg piece.

12. The next step is to cut these arcs out. Secure one leg piece to the work surface using a clamp, positioning the clamp opposite the top of the arc. Make sure the arc is completely free of the work surface.

13. You'll make the cuts using an electric jigsaw. Position the jigsaw at one end of the arc, with the blade on the waste side of the line, but not touching the wood. Turn on the saw. Move the saw slowly and steadily forward, keeping its bottom held flat against the surface of the wood. Don't tilt the machine or move too fast. When you reach the tip of the arc, stop, and turn the machine off. When the blade stops moving, pull the saw free of the wood.

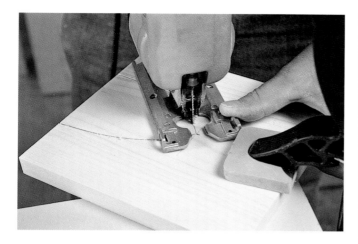

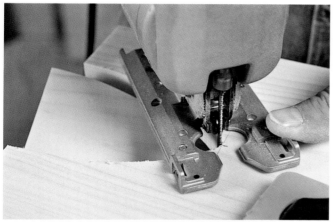

14. Move the jigsaw to the other side of the arc and cut the other side until the excess piece falls free.

15. Repeat the process on the other leg piece.

16. Use 120-grade sandpaper to smooth out the curves, by hand or with an orbital sander. Either way, sand both the inside of the arc as well as the outside surface, as shown here. Put the two bench legs aside.

17. Next, you will cut two rectangular grooves—called dados—into the underside of the seat of the bench. These grooves will accept the bench legs. To mark off the cuts, measure in $1\,^1/_2$ inches from both of the short sides of the bench seat.

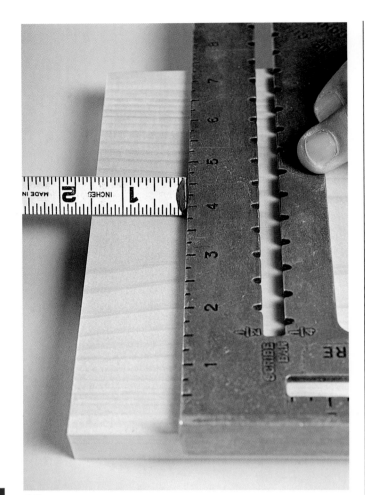

18. Use a square to help you draw straight lines through the marks, parallel to the short sides of the bench seat.

19. Use two clamps to secure the bench seat to the work surface, lining up the long side of the seat with the edge of the table.

20. Secure a straight-edge clamp exactly 4¹/₂ inches in from the short side of the seat.

21. Select a ³/₄-inch-wide straight-cutting router bit and attach it to the plunge router. Set the depth of the router to ³/₈ inch. (The rule of thumb for choosing a router depth is to make it half the thickness of the wood.) Place the straight edge of the plunge router along the edge of the straight-edge clamp. Notice how the edge of the bit nearest you falls at the penciled line.

Making a Small Bench

22. Position the router so the bit is off the edge of the wood.

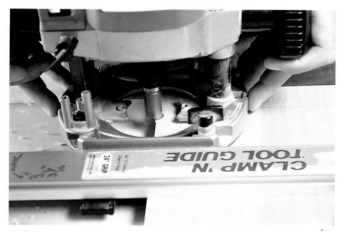

23. Turn the router on, lower the bit, and move it along the guide. Keep the straight edge of the router pressed against the guide as you cut the groove.

24. Continue the cut until the bit is clear of the wood. Turn the router off.

25. The finished cut should look like this.

26. Now cut a dado on the other side of the bench seat. Again, the guide should be secured exactly $4^{1}/_{2}$ inches from the edge of the seat.

Making a Small Bench

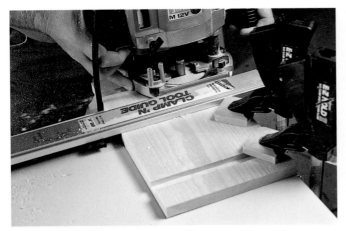

As before, keep the router moving steadily without pressing it too hard into the wood.

27. Test-fit a bench leg into the dado. It should fit snugly.

28. On the top side of the bench seat, measure in $1^7/8$ inches from the short side and make a mark approximately halfway between the two long sides. This will be directly above the center of the dado on the underside.

29. Make two more marks above the dado on both ends of the board, just in from the long side and $1^7/8$ inches from the short side. These marks will show you where to hammer finish nails after the legs have been inserted into the dados.

30. Apply wood glue to one of the dados. Unlike the glue used on the cutting board, the glue for the bench does not have to be 100 percent waterproof. Gloves are not required when using a simple wood glue (but they do help to keep your hands glue-free).

31. Use a small brush to spread the glue across the bottom of the dado.

32. Carefully push the leg into the dado.

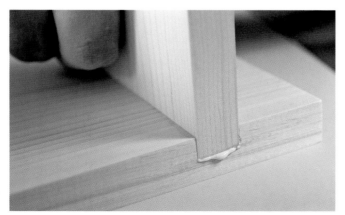

33. A bit of glue may seep out; wipe it away with a cloth or rag.

34. Now glue the other leg in place.

35. Next, before the glue dries, carefully flip the bench over and tap finish nails into the wood at the marks you made. Tap them in just enough so that they are held straight up from the wood. Use a speed square to make certain that the legs are perfectly perpendicular to the bench seat. Adjust the legs if necessary.

Tips on Hammering

Hammering nails into wood is one of the most common tasks in woodworking (and lots of other household projects). There is a proper way to wield a hammer. Grip it in the middle of the handle, but don't squeeze it. A good hammering motion uses a lot of wrist, a little elbow, and not much shoulder. Hit the nail with the center of the hammer head. The surface of the head that strikes the nail should be parallel to the surface of the wood when it strikes. Avoid glancing or sideways blows. To hold very small nails, some woodworkers push them through thin cardboard and use the cardboard to hold the nail in place for the first few blows—they're less likely to smash a finger this way.

A common beginner's mistake is to drive nail heads completely into the wood, which leaves unsightly hammer marks on the surface. One way to avoid this is to use finish nails with a nail set.

36. Now hammer in the finish nails. See the sidebar for more details on hammering technique.

37. After your initial hammering, the heads of the finish nails should protrude slightly, as shown here.

38. Place a nail set on the nail head and lightly tap the set with a hammer to drive the nail head completely below the surface of the wood.

39. The small hole that's left will be filled in later.

40. Flip the bench over. The legs should be 9 1/2 inches apart, which is how long the crosspiece will be.

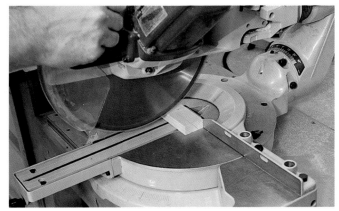

41. Use the miter saw to cut your 1 1/2-inch wide, 18-inch long piece down to a length of 9 1/2 inches. (Pictured here is an extra 1 1/2-by-14-inch piece from Step 5 being cut down to 9 1/2 inches.)

42. Sand this piece with 120-grade paper.

43. Test-fit the crosspiece between the bench legs.

44. The crosspiece should be 3³/₈ inches from the edge of the legs on both sides . . .

. . . and 1¹/₂ inches up from the underside of the seat. Measure both ends of the crosspiece.

45. When the crosspiece is correctly positioned, make a few small pencil marks to indicate the placement.

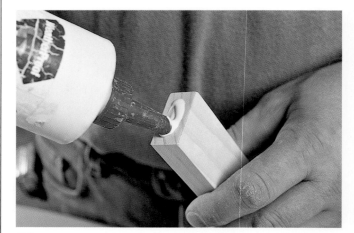

46. Take the crosspiece out and apply glue to both ends.

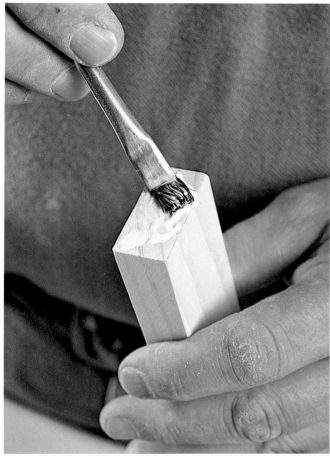

47. Use your finger or a small brush to spread the glue.

48. Put the crosspiece back in between the legs. Position it properly, using your marks for guidance.

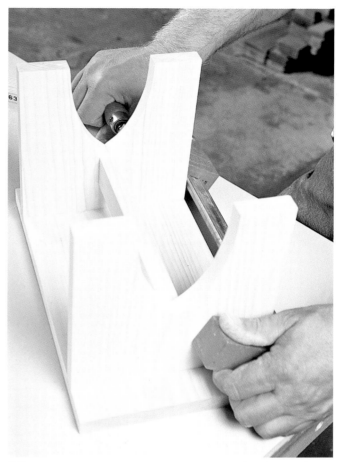

49. Use a clamp to hold the crosspiece firmly in place as the glue dries.

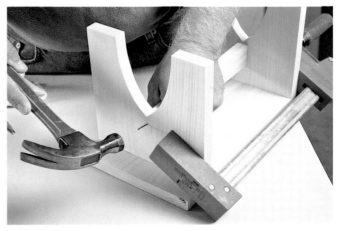

50. Two finish nails driven into both ends of the crosspiece will offer further stability after the glue dries. Place each nail below the top of the arc, near the center of the end of the crosspiece.

51. Use a nail set to tap the nail heads below the surface of the wood.

52. The last step in assembling the small bench is to add the side pieces. Apply glue along one long side of the bench seat.

53. Spread the glue evenly along the wood surface.

54. Press one of the 14-inch-long, 1 1/2-inch-wide pieces onto the long side of the bench seat, making certain that the top of the side piece is aligned evenly with the top of the seat.

55. Hammer finish nails into the side piece to hold it in place. Four evenly spaced nails per side should do the trick. Set the nails. Now glue and hammer the opposite side piece into place. Wipe away any oozing glue. Let the glue dry.

56. Next, you'll need to round over the edges of the bench. Use a router fitted with a ³/₈-inch roundover bit. Place the bit near one of the bench sides, right at the corner, but not touching the wood.

57. Turn the machine on and slowly but steadily move the router along the edge, pushing it away from you.

58. Round over all four edges of the bench.

59. After routing is complete, the bench should look like this.

60. To finish the bench, you will fill in all the nail holes with wood filler. Choose a light-colored filler for light woods, dark for dark woods. A birch wood filler is used here.

61. Using a flat stick, press a small amount of filler into the holes and smear it across the top of the hole.

62. Then, with the stick, scrape off the excess filler, being careful not to pull the rest out of the hole. Let the filler dry and harden for the recommended time.

63. To prepare the stool for painting, sand it completely with 120-grade paper, followed by 220-grade paper. Either hand or orbital sanding will work.

Making a Small Bench

Painting

There are all kinds of paints for all kinds of surfaces—indoor, outdoor, latex, oil-based, paints for wood, paints for glass, paints for metal . . . the list is extensive. Before you buy a can of paint, read the label to make certain you're getting what you need.

Stir the paint thoroughly before you begin. Load up the brush, then tap it against the top of the container so you don't drip paint onto the wood surface. Then begin painting with long, smooth strokes. Experts recommend that, once you have begun, you paint from dry areas into painted ones. Reload the brush as often as you need to—don't scrub to get every last bit of paint out of the brush. When you think you're done, before you put the paint away, look over the entire project carefully in good light. Chances are you missed a spot.

Using a good paintbrush is important. A cheap one will shed, and you'll spend a lot of time plucking stray bristles out of wet paint. Before you buy, give the bristles a tug. If you can pull any out, put the brush back on the rack. Disposable sponge brushes won't shed, are inexpensive, and work well for smaller projects.

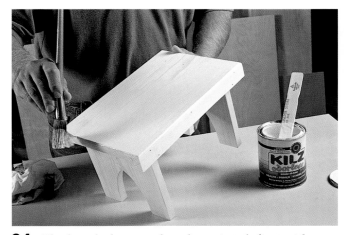

64. The bench then needs to be painted, first with primer, then with wood paint. Before painting, use a tack cloth to remove all dust. Then paint all the surfaces with primer and let dry completely; see the sidebar for guidance on painting wood. When the bench is thoroughly dry, sand it once more with 220-grade paper, then remove the dust with a tack cloth. A final coat of paint completes the project. If the final paint color is relatively dark, such as the green used in the example on page 35, you might need to use two coats.

4

Making a Peg Shelf

- Creating a symmetrical curved design
- Cutting a plywood template
- Routing a curved edge
- Drilling straight holes
- Affixing pegs to a wooden shelf
- Staining and varnishing

Building this attractive and useful shelf will introduce a number of new woodworking skills and, in the case of the curved back piece, will allow you to exercise some creativity.

Start with a finished piece of wood that is 50 inches long, $5^{1}/_{2}$ inches wide, and $^{3}/_{4}$ inch thick. A piece of red oak was used here—its wonderful red color is highlighted by the stain and varnish finish applied at the end of the project. Matching red oak pegs $3^{1}/_{2}$ inches long and $^{7}/_{8}$ inch wide and red oak plugs were used as well.

Making a Peg Shelf

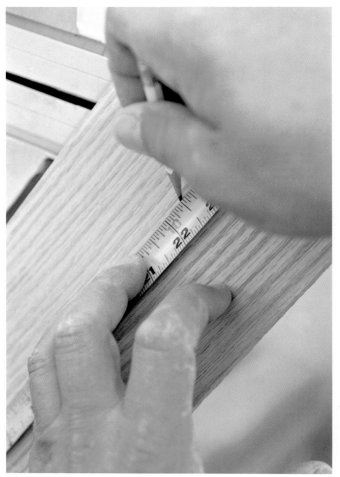

1. Measure 22¹/₂ inches in from a short edge of the wood and make a pencil mark.

2. Draw a straight line through the 22¹/₂-inch mark and cut the wood along the line using a power miter saw.

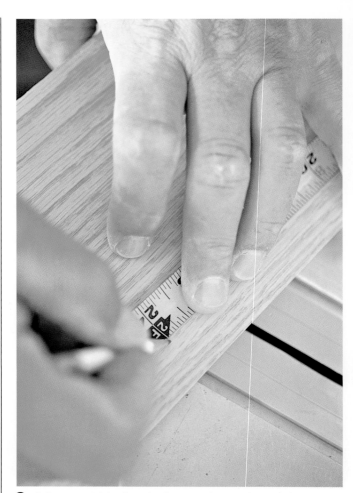

3. Measure 24 inches in from a short edge of the original piece of wood and draw another line.

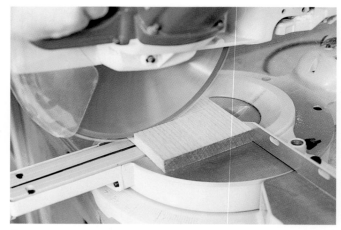

4. Cut the wood along the 24-inch line using the miter saw. The 24-inch piece of wood will form the shelf; the 22¹/₂-inch piece will form the shelf back.

54

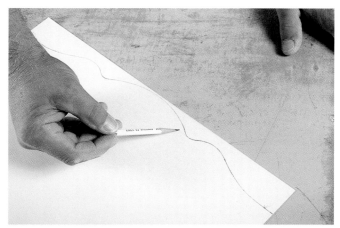

5. You'll next create a design for the shelf back. Use the French curve to create a curved line on a heavy piece of paper, such as poster board or oak tag. The curved line must cover a length of 22 1/2 inches and will serve as the edge of a paper template that will be used to transfer the design to a piece of plywood. The design shown here is symmetrical, which is a good choice for a project of this kind. An easy way to make a symmetrical design is to draw a curved line that covers a length of 11 1/4 inches, cut it out, trace it onto a piece of heavy paper, then flip the cut piece and continue the line. For this project, the curved edge shouldn't be more than 5 inches from its lowest point to its highest point.

7. Place the paper template on top of a piece of plywood that's 22 1/2 inches long and 1/4 inch thick. Trace along the curved edge. Remove the paper.

8. Clamp the plywood firmly to the work surface so that the curved line hangs over the edge.

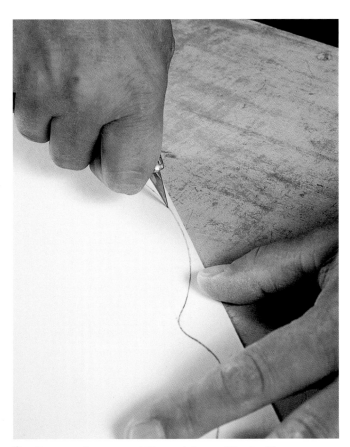

6. Cut out the curved line with a utility knife.

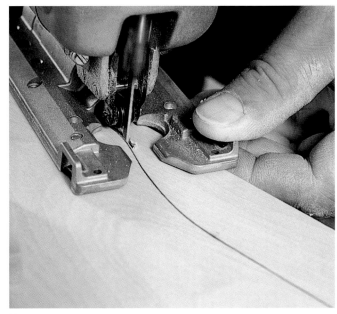

9. Use an electric jigsaw to cut out the design.

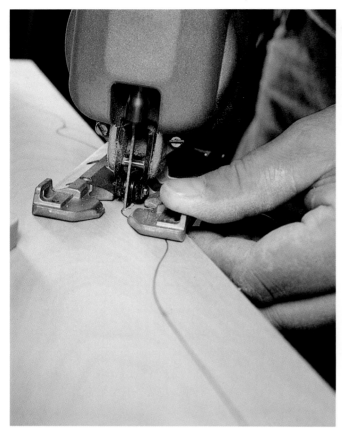

The more complex your design, the more careful your sawing will have to be.

10. After the plywood is cut, release the wood from the clamps. This is your template, which you will use to transfer the curved design to the good wood.

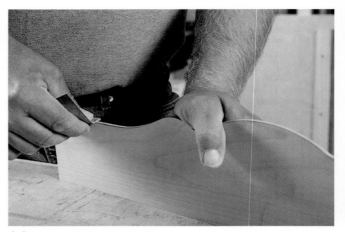

11. Sand the cut edge of the plywood with 120-grade paper.

12. Place the plywood template on top of the 22$\frac{1}{2}$-inch piece of wood, aligning bottom and side edges.

13. Clamp both pieces of wood to the work surface.

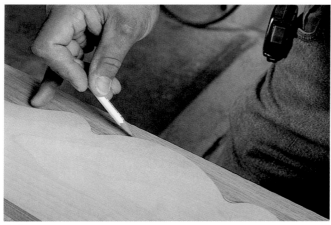

14. Trace the curved outline of the template onto the wood.

15. Release the wood from the clamps and remove the plywood.

16. Clamp only the good wood to the work surface with the pencil line hanging off the table edge.

17. Position the blade of the jigsaw along the edge of the wood about $^1/_{16}$ inch away from the pencil line on the waste side of the wood.

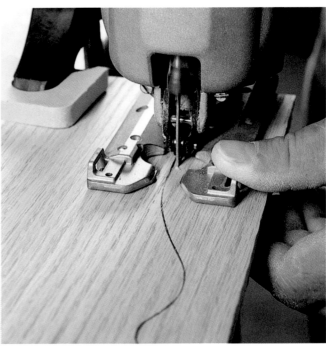

18. Begin cutting the wood, following the curve of the drawn line.

Maintain a distance of $^1/_{16}$ inch from the line for the entire cut.

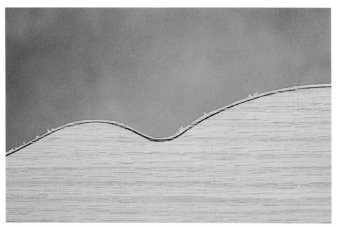

19. This finished cut should look like this.

20. Next, place the plywood template over the cut wood as shown.

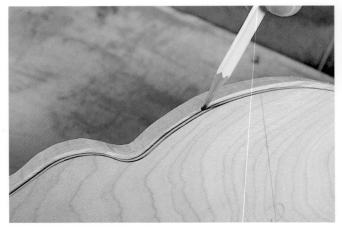

21. You don't need to draw a line—the pencil here is simply illustrating the $^1/_{16}$-inch gap between the edge of the template and the edge of the wood beneath it. You will need to use a router to cut a smooth edge that follows the template's line exactly.

22. Clamp the two pieces of wood to the work surface once again, making sure the straight edges of both pieces are aligned.

23. A router and a straight-cutting pattern bit (shown here) will be used to cut the excess $^1/_{16}$ inch off of the wood and make it smooth. The pattern bit has a guide bearing that will ride against the edge of the plywood template as the bit cuts.

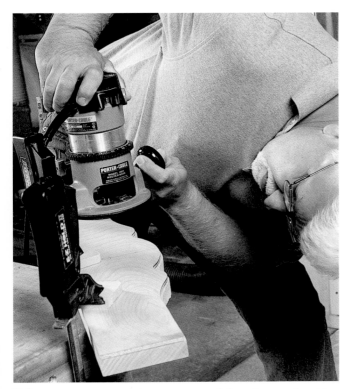

24. Place the router base on top of the plywood, with the bit off to one side and the bit's guide bearing near the template's edge. Don't touch the wood with the bit until the router is turned on.

25. Turn the router on, move the bit into position, and move the tool slowly and steadily along the curved edge.

As the bit's guide rides along the edge, the spinning blade cuts away the overhanging wood.

Keep the router base flat as you cut—don't tilt or lift the machine.

26. When you're finished cutting, turn off the machine. Remove the wood from the clamps. Here is what you should have—an almost perfectly smooth edge needing only a bit of sanding.

27. Measure in 4 1/2 inches from a short edge of the routed piece and make a mark.

28. Measure 9 inches in from the same end of the piece and make a mark. Repeat this process from the other end—4 1/2 and then 9 inches in.

29. Use a square to mark vertical lines through all four marks.

30. Measure 1³/₄ inches up from the bottom (the straight edge) of the piece, along one of the vertical lines, and make a mark.

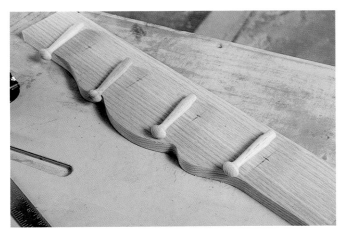

31. Make a 1³/₄-inch mark at each of the other three vertical lines. The Xs indicate where the shelf's four pegs will go. The marks should all be 4¹/₂ inches apart.

32. A forstner drill bit will be used to cut the holes that will accept the pegs—make sure that the diameter of the bit matches the pegs you use. The holes need to be ¹/₂ inch deep. Measure up ¹/₂ inch from the tip of the bit and wrap a piece of masking tape around the bit to indicate the distance. The bottom edge of the tape should be exactly ¹/₂ inch from the tip of the bit.

33. Attach the forstner bit to an electric drill. Place the bit over one of the Xs so that the center of the X is directly below the center of the bit. Line the drill up against a square as shown so the drill is perfectly perpendicular to the wood. Don't touch the wood with the drill bit until the drill is turned on.

34. Turn the drill on and press the bit straight into the wood. Stop when the bottom edge of the tape reaches the surface of the wood. Turn the drill off. Pull the bit out of the hole.

35. The result should be a smooth ½-inch-deep hole.

36. Drill the three other holes the same way.

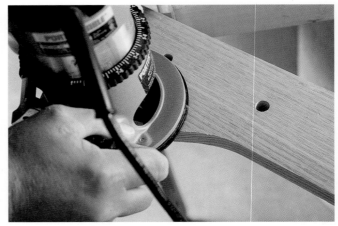

37. The next step is to round over the curved edge of the shelf back. Clamp the back onto the work surface and use a router fitted with a ³/₈-inch roundover bit to round over the piece all along the curve.

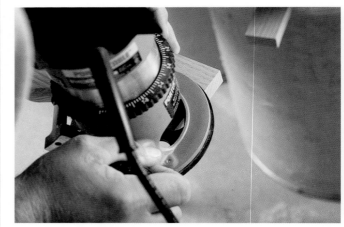

38. Move slowly and steadily, letting the router ride along the edge of the wood.

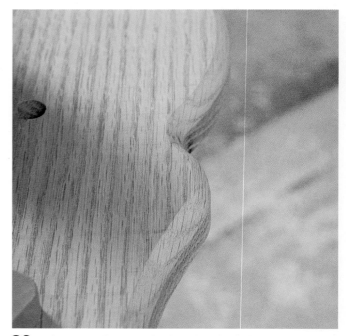

39. The smooth, round edge should follow the curve.

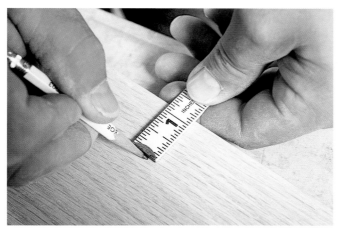

40. Set the curved piece aside. Take the 24-inch piece, measure in 1$\frac{3}{16}$ inches from one of the long edges, and make a mark.

41. Make a line the full length of the 24-inch piece that is 1$\frac{3}{16}$ inches away from the straight edge. You can do this using a combination square by holding the tip of a pencil along the edge of the tool and moving it down the length of the piece, keeping the guide pressed along the wood's edge. This line shows where the shelf's plate groove will eventually go, at the back of the shelf.

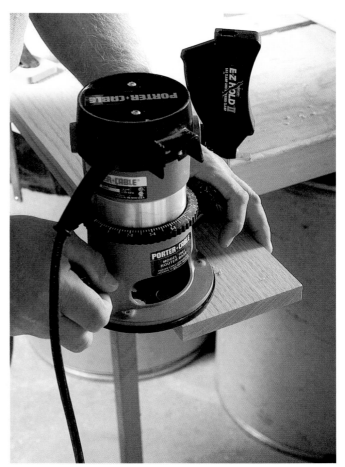

42. Next, clamp the 24-inch shelf to the edge of the work surface. Use a router fitted with a $\frac{3}{8}$-inch round-over bit to round over the two short edges and the front of the shelf, but not the back. Keep the back edge square.

43. The 24-inch-long line indicates the edge of the shelf's plate groove. To make the groove, secure a straight-edge clamp with its edge 4 inches in from the back of the shelf. The plunge router will ride along this edge as it cuts the groove.

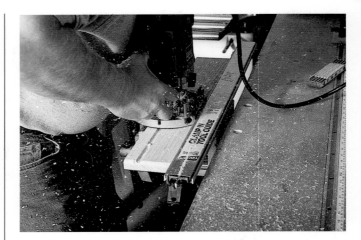

44. Secure the wood—with the straight-edge clamp attached—to the edge of the work surface using a vise. A piece of scrap wood placed between the shelf and the vice jaw will protect the shelf's surface.

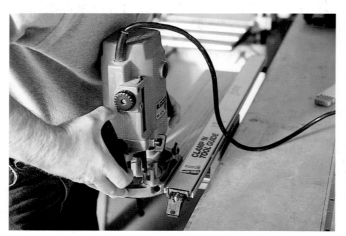

45. Attach a convex radius bit to the plunge router. Place the bit off the edge of one of the short ends and set the router guide up against the edge of the straight-edge clamp.

46. Turn the router on and move it slowly and steadily down the length of the wood, keeping it pressed against the guide. When the blade clears the wood, turn the machine off.

47. This is the finished groove. Notice how it starts and ends off the edges of the shelf.

The convex radius bit cuts a shallow, curved groove.

48. From a short, rounded edge of the shelf, in the small space between the back edge and the groove, use a combination square to measure in 2 inches and make a mark.

49. Next, measure $^3/_8$ inch in from the long rounded edge and make a mark that crosses the mark you made previously. The X indicates where you will drill a hole for a wood screw to attach the shelf and the shelf back.

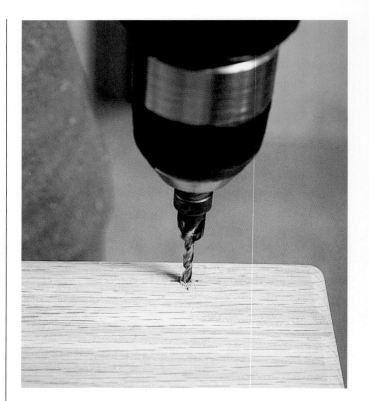

50. Make marks all the way down the length of the shelf—they should be 5 inches apart from one another and ³⁄₈ inch in from the long rounded edge. Like the first mark, the last one should be 2 inches from the short edge of the shelf.

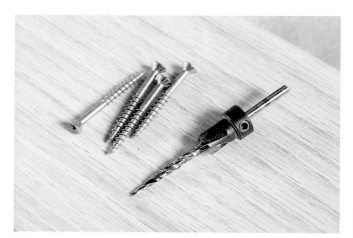

51. Next, you will drill holes at each of the five marks using a tapered drill bit and a countersink (shown here with wood screws).

52. Drill through the first mark and countersink far enough to place the head of a 1¹⁄₄-inch flathead screw below the surface of the wood.

53. Do the same for the remaining marks.

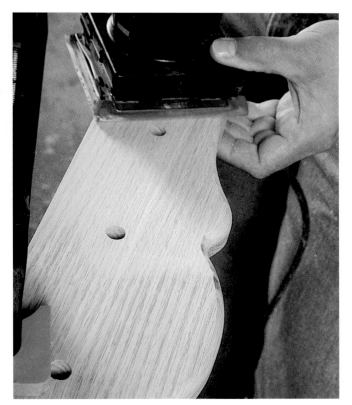

54. After the holes are drilled, sand both the shelf and shelf back. Use 120-grade paper, followed by 220-grade paper.

Make certain you sand the entire surface of both pieces, including the edges.

55. When you're finished sanding, wipe off the wood with a tack cloth. Then, clamp the shelf back, straight-edge-up, against the work surface using the vise. Make certain that at least $^3/_4$ inch of the shelf back is sticking up past the surface of the table.

56. Apply glue to the straight edge (it doesn't have to be 100 percent waterproof glue). Place the shelf on the back, carefully lining up the back edges of the two pieces. The groove goes nearest the shelf back. There should be an equal amount of overhang on either side of the shelf. You may wish to measure in $^3/_4$ inch from both short sides of the shelf and mark lines on the underside to aid in placing it on the back.

57. Drive 1¹/₄-inch flathead wood screws into the five holes.

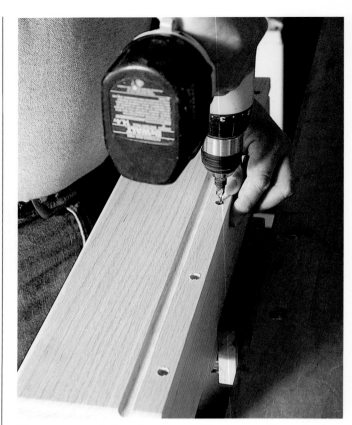

The screws and the glue—once it's dry—will guarantee that the shelf will be sturdy and won't buckle under pressure.

The screw heads should be below the wood surface, at the bottom of the countersink.

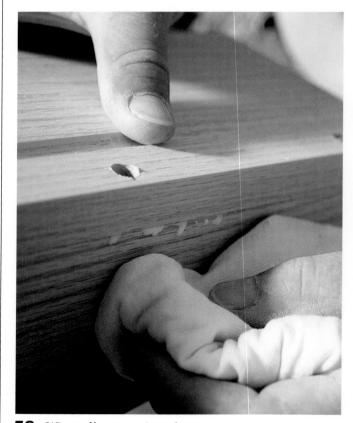

58. Wipe off any oozing glue.

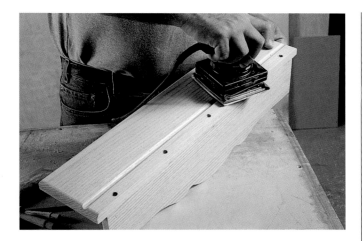

60. Next, squeeze out a dollop of wood glue onto a piece of scrap paper or wood.

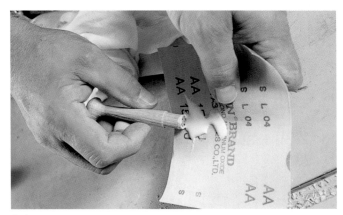

61. Roll the ends of the four shelf pegs in the glue.

59. Once the glue is dry, sand the entire piece once again using 220-grade paper and wipe it off with a tack cloth.

62. Insert the pegs into the holes and wipe away any excess glue.

63. Very gently tap the pegs into the holes with a hammer to make certain they are firmly in place.

65. Insert the plugs into the screw holes.

64. Now dip five wooden plugs in the glue, covering their bottoms and sides.

66. Gently tap the plugs in place. Once the glue is dry, another sanding of the entire shelf with 220-grade paper will ensure a smooth surface. After sanding, wipe the shelf with a tack cloth.

67. The next step will be to stain the wood. Put on a pair of gloves and gently stir the stain with a piece of scrap wood.

68. Dip a lint-free cloth into the stain.

Staining

In addition to helping to preserve woodworking projects, stain also adds color to wood and brings out its naturally occurring patterns. For experienced woodworkers, staining can be an elaborate process, involving careful color mixing, multiple coats, and so on. For the beginner, however, the following should suffice.

As you might expect, spilled stain is not easy to remove. It's a good idea to spread out plenty of newspaper and put on a pair of gloves before staining. In order to ensure uniform thickness, stain must first be properly agitated by shaking or stirring— mix for longer than you might think necessary, since consistent application is a high priority for any staining job.

Stain should be applied with a brush or lint-free cloth that is completely clean. Residue from oil, paint, or other substances may interfere with the effectiveness of the stain. Likewise, the wood surface must be totally clear and unfinished. It's recommended that you give your project a thorough sanding before using stain.

Because stain is absorbed into the wood rather than coating it, you have some freedom in how you apply the stain—you can go with, against, or at an angle to the grain. Just be sure your application is even over the entire surface of the piece, or unsightly variations in the color of the wood may result. You may find that, despite your best efforts, the ends of your project take on a darker color than the rest of the piece. This often occurs because the end of a board has large, open pores (the "end grain") that soak up more stain than the rest of the wood. You can sometimes avoid this by sanding the end grain with a finer sandpaper than you use for the rest of the piece.

69. Apply the stain evenly over the entire piece and let it dry thoroughly for at least 24 hours. If you choose, you can then further preserve and protect your shelf by applying a finish such as a varnish or a lacquer.

Resources

BOOKS

Classics From the New Yankee Workshop
by Norm Abrams (Little, Brown Publishers, 1990)

Complete Book of Woodworking
(North American Affinity Books, 2002)

Complete Illustrated Guide to Shaping Wood
by Lonnie Bird (Taunton Press, 2001)

New Wood Finishing Book
by Michael Dresdner (Taunton Press, 1999)

The Table Saw Book
by Kelly Mehler (Taunton Press, 2003)

Understanding Wood, Second Edition
by R. Bruce Hoadley (Taunton Press, 2000)

MAGAZINES

American Woodworker

Fine Woodworking

Popular Woodworking

Woodworker's Journal